All Your Property Tax Questions: Answered

Tax saving strategies all savvy property investors and developers need to know

by Reza Hooda FCA CTA

First published April 2019 by: Reza Hooda

Design by: Steven Baldwin, **www.Noir-Designs.co.uk**

Paperback ISBN: 978-1-9161049-0-7

www.allaboutpropertytax.com

DEDICATION

To my dear wife Farzana and four wonderful children
Zayn-Ali, Kareem, Safeeya & Raheem. I love you all

Contents

About the Author

Reza is a qualified chartered accountant and chartered tax advisor. He started his career with PwC advising Entrepreneurs and Private Clients on their corporate and personal tax affairs.

He bought into his current firm Walji & Co in 2008 and has since built up a successful accountancy practice as the Managing Partner with a particular specialism for clients engaged in anything property related. This ranges from individuals with property portfolios, property developers and Entrepreneurs who diversify into property using the profits from profitable trading companies.

Furthermore, Reza has personal experience in building and managing a multi million pound property portfolio consisting of both commercial and residential properties in the Hampshire area. One of his recent projects included the acquisition of a series of commercial units and undertaking conversion of offices on the upper floors to 18 residential apartments under permitted development planning rules. The total value of the finished development was £5.5m generating an ROI of 50% within 18m.

With both the technical expertise and personal experience of being a property investor himself, Reza can add real value to his property clients' affairs.

Introduction

The last few years have seen an unprecedented wave of legislation introduced by the government adversely affecting property investors and developers.

Most notable has been the removal of mortgage interest relief coupled with an additional 3% stamp duty charge on second (and further additional) properties. Both have no doubt had an impact on the property market.

Add to that the removal of the wear and tear allowance which was worth 10% of gross rentals as a tax deduction on furnished properties.

Those three measures have certainly taken the steam out of the buy-to-let market. In recent times fewer buy-to-let mortgages have been approved and with that a lower number of landlords have entered the market.

This has certainly dampened the ability for new buy-to-let investors to enter the market.

It has also deterred the amateur landlords for whom the promise of an easy passive income through property is no longer a sure thing. However, this new environment presents seasoned property investors with a potential buying opportunity.

This book presents 14 chapters answering the most common questions I receive from property investors and developers. I expand into explaining tax saving strategies targeted at those savvy property investors and developers for whom there will always be a market. It also aims to create awareness of tax-planning tips to mitigate the burden of punitive changes in the tax code.

I hope you find this book useful. If you would like to find out more about working with me, please refer to the next section entitled 'How you can work with me.'

Warm regards

Reza Hooda, FCA CTA
Property Tax Expert & Investor

www.allaboutpropertytax.com

How you can work with me

You can connect with me on LinkedIn or on Twitter @rezahooda where I regularly post useful articles and blogs on property tax saving.

If you have bought this book or downloaded the free pdf copy, you will be on the mailing list to receive property tax saving tips on a regular basis. If you have been given this book, you can get on the mailing list by visiting www.allaboutpropertytax.com and downloading the free e-book or you can email **karen@walji.uk.com**.

If you would like to arrange a tailored meeting to discuss your specific property circumstances then I normally work via what I call a Strategic Consultation.

These consultations are paid for in advance and are tailored to your circumstances and answering your specific property questions. It can be either face to face at my office near Southampton or via a video / phone call.

At the end of this consultation one of three things will happen:

1. you'll take away the knowledge from the consultation and implement
2. we'll agree to work together
3. you'll ask for a full refund on the basis that the consultation was of no use to you whatsoever; I've never had to write a cheque but it's there for peace of mind.

Your small investment for this consultation is £279+vat.

To book a slot please contact my PA Karen Hankins on 02380 610 573 or by email at **karen@walji.uk.com** with Strategic Consultation as the subject title.

Chapter 1

Which Structure Do I Go With?

The most common question now asked by those buying investment property is this: do I take the limited company route or buy in my own name?

The answer is – as with most things in tax – it depends!

It depends on a number of factors.

The most important among them is what you want to achieve by choosing to invest in property.

You could be planning to:

- build a portfolio of properties from which to generate a passive income
- invest with a view to add value to a property that you then intend to sell to earn a profit that you will reinvest in other property
- Invest your life savings in property to give you a pension for your retirement.

Whatever the objective, it's important to have this clarity at the outset so that the structure you choose is tailored to your needs and gives you the best results.

WHAT HAS CHANGED?

As we saw in the introduction there were three main changes to the tax treatment of rental income that have adversely affected all buy-to-let property owners. These are:

1. Introduction of 3% stamp-duty surcharge
2. Abolition of 10% wear and tear allowance
3. Removal of tax relief for mortgage interest

Let's look at each point in some more detail.

Introduction of 3% stamp duty surcharge

In April 2016 the government introduced a 3% surcharge on any purchase of a second property by an individual.

This was done within a political context to give the impression to the public that the government is doing something about the country's housing crisis.

How attacking the very people who provide most of the rented-housing stock achieves this is a debate for another day.

The surcharge applies to anyone who already has an interest in a property in the UK.

This means that a husband and wife (or those in a civil partnership) jointly owning a property would be deemed to have an interest in that asset. Therefore either party would be subject to the 3% surcharge if they bought a second property.

Provision has been made for those buying a new home whilst being unable to sell their old home.

In that scenario, the surcharge still needs to be paid but it can be recovered provided the old home is sold within 18 months of moving into a new home.

This is not ideal as it means parting with extra cash at the point of completion – money that is naturally in short supply when dealing with the huge investment of moving home.

Does the 3% surcharge apply to companies?

As a limited company is considered to have legal status in its own right, it's not unreasonable to think that a company should be exempt from stamp duty for the first property it buys.

Sadly, tax legislation does not always follow common sense. Companies are subject to the 3% surcharge from their first property investment regardless of the property ownership position of the company's shareholders.

Abolition of 10% wear and tear allowance

The other main factor when looking at whether to hold property personally or via a limited company is the removal of the wear and tear allowance.

Before tax year 2016/17 this provided a flat 10% tax allowance on rental of a furnished property, making it hugely favourable for landlords renting property on this basis.

It meant that landlords, without spending money on replacing furniture or other items, could claim a fixed 10% of gross rents against their rental profits.

The impact this has had on landlords operating property either personally or in a partnership was substantial.

Consider a portfolio generating rental income of £100,000 and profits after expenses of £80,000.

The wear and tear allowance would have given an additional £8,000 expense to be offset against the rental profit. For a higher rate taxpayer this would be worth 40% of £8,000.

On that basis the annual tax bill of a higher-rate taxpayer would have increased by £3,200 on the same amount of rental profit.

That essentially reduces the gross rental yield earned from the portfolio by 3.2 percentage points. That has a dramatic impact on the return on investment.

The ability therefore to retain profits in the company and only pay tax at the lower corporate rates (currently 19%) is one of the most compelling reasons to hold a property through a limited company.

Removal of tax relief for mortgage interest

The changes mean that any mortgage interest paid on a loan taken out to buy an investment property is no longer deductible as a taxable expense starting in tax year 2020/21 for a higher rate taxpayer.

Up to then there is a phased withdrawal of the relief starting in tax year 2016/17.

This restriction on mortgage-interest relief will significantly increase tax payable for higher-rate taxpayers.

Basic-rate taxpayers who are close to the higher-rate threshold will also be affected because of how the calculation works.

It's relatively complicated, so let's explain by way of an example.

Say you have a modest portfolio of buy-to-lets that you have grown with the help of finance.

On secured loans of £1 million you are probably paying annual interest of around £40,000 assuming a 4% interest rate.

Previously this interest would have been fully allowable to you as an expense of your rental business. If you are a higher rate taxpayer, this 'expense' would be worth 40% of £40,000 i.e. £16,000 in cash terms as your tax bill is being reduced by that amount.

Let's see how that will change from 2020/21 using an example with the above figures and showing the comparison between the old and new rules:

Old rules

Gross rental income	**£70,000**
Mortgage interest	(£40,000)
Other costs	(£5,000)
Profit	£25,000
Tax as BR taxpayer (20%)	£5,000
Tax as HR taxpayer (40%)	£10,000
Tax as TR taxpayer (45%)	£11,250

The above table shows the position for all taxpayers based on the old rules where mortgage interest was allowable in full.

Now let's look at the impact of the new rules once they are fully in force from 2020/21.

New rules

Gross rental income	**£70,000**
Mortgage interest	not deductible
Other costs	(£5,000)
Profit	£65,000
Tax on Profit as BR taxpayer (20%)	£13,000
Allowable deduction for interest at basic rate i.e. £40,000 @ 20%	(£8,000)
Tax payable	**£5,000 – no change**
Tax on Profit as HR taxpayer (40%)	£26,000
Allowable deduction for interest at basic rate i.e. £40,000 @ 20%	(£8,000)
Tax payable	£18,000 – increase of 80%
Tax as TR taxpayer (45%)	£29,250
Allowable deduction for interest at basic rate i.e £40,000 @ 20%	(£8,000)
Tax payable	£21,250 – increase of 89%

Therefore In the example above, your annual tax bill as a higher or top rate taxpayer could increase by as much as **89%**.

This removal represents a significant tax hike for any landlord with a leveraged portfolio. It also means that the expected return on investment or yield on the property also drops. This should be taken into account when undertaking the appraisal for a new property purchase via leverage.

This presents a compelling reason to switch towards ownership of property via a limited company.

However, if you're buying property with cash then this interest relief is not applicable or relevant to you, therefore the choice between personal or limited company ownership depends on other factors.

"It's important to have clarity at the outset so that the structure you choose is tailored to your needs and gives you the best results."

SO, HOW DOES HOLDING PROPERTY THROUGH A LIMITED COMPANY HELP?

There are four main ways why holding property through a company is beneficial:

1. Ability to deduct mortgage interest in full
2. Rental profits taxed at lower corporation tax rates (currently 19%, falling to 17% by 2020)
3. Flexible distribution of profits to shareholders

4. Retention of profits for re-investment

The main advantage is the ability of companies still to deduct mortgage interest *in full* compared to the restriction for individuals holding property directly.

So for those landlords who have *high debt-servicing costs* or who are looking to expand their portfolio through refinance and leverage, *the company structure is more favourable.*

The company can deduct interest paid on loans in full and offset against its rental profits.

The other advantage of the company ownership route is the ability for the company to retain its profits.

As the company is a separate legal entity, it pays tax on its own profits which are then available for distribution to the owners / shareholders.

The shareholders can *choose for their profits to stay in the company*, meaning that the tax suffered on those profits is limited to the lower corporation tax rates of 19% (falling to 17%).

The *benefit of this is that the company then has extra cash funds available to reinvest* in other properties to expand the portfolio further.

This is *highly advantageous to the landlord looking to grow the portfolio* and minimise the amount of cash that is lost through tax.

By contrast individuals holding property personally would pay tax at up to 45% whether or not they need use of the rental income for re-investment.

Whilst retaining profits in the company is useful to those who are looking perhaps to expand their portfolio or don't need the income from the properties, it may not suit those individuals who need an income from their properties.

This is a further consideration when determining whether the limited company route is right for you.

(We'll look at the implications of extracting funds from a company in a later chapter)

DOWNSIDES OF HOLDING PROPERTY THROUGH A COMPANY

One of the main reasons why property was not typically held through a company before these changes was the *potential double taxation that arises on sale of a property* in the company and having access to the sale proceeds.

As a company is its own legal entity, it pays corporation tax on profits *and capital gains* from disposals of assets.

The company would be liable for corporation tax on the increase in value of the property from the time it was bought to the time it was sold.

Thereafter if you wanted to withdraw that cash from the company for personal use, you would need to extract those funds via a dividend or salary etc.

The difference in the effective rates of tax of the two methods is shown in the example below.

Example:

Property bought for £200,000 and sold for £300,000 a few years later.

At current capital gains tax rates the difference in holding this property personally compared to through a company would be:

	Personal	Company
Gain subject to tax	100,000	100,000
CGT @ 28%	28,000	
Corp tax @ 19%		19,000
Income tax @ 32.5%		26,325
Cash in hand	72,000	54,675
Effective tax rate	28%	45.3%

The above example is based on the tax that applies to a higher-rate taxpayer. It's based on the assumption that all the proceeds are extracted in one lump sum and in the same tax year.

It's possible that the proceeds are extracted over a longer period, which would be beneficial and minimise the tax if you do not need access to all the proceeds straight away.

What's more, if the funds are re-invested then the tax rate that applies to the company of only 19% (falling to 17%) means greater funds available for re-investment.

Finance arrangements

In the past it has been more difficult to obtain finance for buy to let properties via a company. Lenders have preferred landlords to buy in their own name which helps the lender as the landlord is effectively personally liable for any default.

However given the tax changes that have taken place and more and more landlords making the shift to holding properties via a company, lenders have had to adapt their credit policy and products to remain active and competitive. As such there is no real difference now in the buy to let products available for individuals and companies.

SUMMARY

The introduction of the punitive tax changes recently has made the proposition of *buying properties through a limited company more favourable.*

Previously the limited company route was not that popular and was mainly the preserve of larger property investors, mainly because of the double taxation charge on taking property out of the portfolio and inflexible buy to let mortgage products.

However, with the changes, especially the removal of the wear and tear allowance and the phasing out of mortgage-interest relief, the limited company route has certainly become more appealing.

In summary, the limited company route is without doubt the way to go for property investors who:

- want to grow a portfolio
- plan to retain a profit within the company in order to buy further properties
- do not necessarily need all the income and profit that the portfolio generates.

For those who still need income from properties to live on then it may be worth doing some extra calculations to see if a limited company would be the most efficient route for you.

The table below explores whether the company route is preferable depending on your objectives. Clearly this is only an indication and you should seek proper advice based on your circumstances.

More favourable	Less favourable
Looking to build a portfolio for long term	Main source of income for living
Do not need main source of income from portfolio	Looking to make a development gain and use for personal purposes e.g. buy main residence
Want to maximise cash available for re-investment	
Looking to leverage portfolio for maximum growth and returns	Buying with cash
Building a portfolio for retirement	
Can introduce family members to maximise tax efficiency on profit distribution	
Undertaking development works with higher risk	

The question of whether to transfer existing properties held personally into a company needs further consideration. We'll look at this in more detail later in the book.

Chapter 2

What expenses can I claim?

Property entrepreneurs or buy-to-let investors often ask what they can or cannot claim against their rental income.

Firstly, we see many property owners *miss out on valuable tax relief* because they're not aware of the full range of expenses they can claim against rental profits.

In a nutshell, *any expenses that are wholly and exclusively incurred for running your property business are deductible against your rental income.* The most common expenses that are probably being claimed already are mortgage interest, maintenance & repair bills and any other obvious property-related costs.

The type of expenses that are often underclaimed or are not claimed at all are:

- Travel expenses
- Computer equipment & office expenses
- Use of home as office

Let's look at each of the above in turn.

"Many property owners miss out on valuable tax relief because they're not aware of the full range of expenses they can claim against rental profits."

TRAVEL EXPENSES

Travel expenses are often underclaimed. Inevitably you will need to travel from property to property to check on tenants or even to check on repairs and the general condition of the property etc.
You will also be making trips to see you bank manager, solicitor and accountant throughout the course of year. You may also attend conferences, courses and even visit DIY centres etc all for the purpose of maintaining and improving your property business.

So long as you *keep a mileage log* (very easy these days through smart apps such as MileiQ – www.mileiq.com), you can claim for each mile at 45p against your rental profits.

This is quite a tax efficient way to offset travel expenses and cut the amount of tax you pay on your rental profits.

COMPUTER EQUIPMENT & OFFICE EXPENSES

Other expenses such as computer equipment, mobile phone costs etc used to maintain your property business such as talking to agents, accountants, tenants and sending emails about quotes can justify claiming computer or mobile-phone expenses.

Your accountant's fees for preparing your tax returns and accounts – and hopefully advising you how to mitigate your liability – are also deductible against your profits.

USE OF HOME AS OFFICE

No doubt as a landlord you manage your portfolio without a dedicated office.

You probably *spend time in your own home managing your rental business*: making calls; dealing with paperwork; storing records; receiving and sending emails directly related to the property business.

So it's perfectly legitimate to charge a rent to your property business / company for the use of your home as an office.

This means a *proportion of your home running costs* – utility bills, mortgage interest (on your home), council tax, broadband etc – can be claimed against your rental profits.

What's more if you're operating through a company, the *total of these running costs creates a sum for you to draw tax-free* because you probably have already paid these home expenses personally.

NON-(IMMEDIATELY)-CLAIMABLE EXPENSES

Expenses that generally cannot be claimed are those which are capital in nature.

These are typically *major capital renovation works*, for example fitting a new bathroom, kitchen, flooring etc.

Do make a note of these expenses – or even better ensure they are logged in your accounts as you will be able to get the benefit of these costs when you come to sell the property.

These capital costs can be added to the cost of the property which is deducted from the eventual sale price. This reduces the gain subject to tax and therefore cuts the amount of tax payable.

FURNISHED PROPERTIES – RENEWALS ALLOWANCE

If you own furnished property you will probably be spending money on furniture and fittings on a regular basis.

While the fixed 10% wear and tear allowance for furnished properties has been abolished, it's still possible to claim for furniture on what's called the 'renewal basis'.

This means you can get tax relief *when you replace furniture* (even though they would normally be classed as capital expenses and therefore disallowable) so long as you make the appropriate claim in your tax return.

For example, if you had furnished a property with beds, chairs, tables etc, inevitably they would have a replacement cycle of between 3 to 5 years depending on the wear and tear associated with those items.

So as and when you replace those items you can claim a tax deduction for the cost. The *initial cost, however, for furnishing the property in the first place is not tax deductible.*

It's well worth getting advice when conducting major repairs or renewals to your property to see if they can be structured to qualify for maximum tax relief. Furthermore, invest in a cloud based accounting system that reconciles your bank for each and every £1 that you spend so you never miss out on claimable expenses.

SUMMARY

In summary, if you are a higher or top-rate tax payer then your expenses are potentially worth up to 45% of the total cost in terms of tax saved.

So if you can find £10,000 worth of expenses to claim then that cuts your tax bill by £4,500. This makes it a subject worth talking about with your accountant to make sure you minimise your tax bills as much as possible.

Chapter 3

How can I draw money out of my limited company?

If you have chosen to structure your property portfolio via a limited company then it's worth considering the shareholding structure. The main reason for this is the *ability to extract funds from this company in the most tax-efficient way*.

A limited company is a separate legal entity from you as an individual. It has its own tax status and pays corporation tax on its profits at the prevailing rate – currently 19% and potentially falling to 17% by the year 2020.

This means that any profits after corporation tax has been paid are left in the company available for distribution to its shareholders.

As a shareholder you can withdraw these funds in a variety of ways:

1. Salary
2. Dividend
3. Interest
4. Pension

SALARY

If you take a salary, you need to set up a payroll scheme and pay income tax and PAYE on a monthly basis to HMRC.

Employer's national insurance is payable on salary paid over the basic national insurance (NI) limit.

The advantages of having a salary are that you are entitled to certain benefits by earning years qualifying for NI contributions. Salaries are also fully deductible as expenses against profits.

The salary option is preferable in some situations but, because of the tax cost of using this route to extract all profits, *dividends are usually more tax efficient*.

You can pay salaries for anyone working directly to manage the company's properties. This includes a *reasonable spouse salary to be paid for work done on the property business*.

Another downside of extracting profits by way of salary is cash flow. Tax on salary, or PAYE as it's called, is payable in the month after the salary is taken.

In comparison *tax is only payable twice a year in arrears on dividend payments*.

DIVIDEND

Paying a dividend is another way of extracting profits from a company. Dividends can only be paid from realised profits i.e. profits after all expenses and taxes. A formal process to vote dividends is required to avoid falling foul of the Companies Act.

The tax treatment of dividends depends on a shareholder's personal income position. The tax rates that apply to dividends based on total income are:

First £2,000	0%
Basic rate taxpayer (up to £50,000)	7.5%
Higher rate taxpayer	32.5%
Top rate taxpayer (more than £150,000)	38.1%

Dividends are treated as the top slice of income i.e. when working out which band the dividend should be taxed in, all other income should be considered first.

If you take dividends – the most common way of extracting surplus funds from the company and still the most tax efficient – you can take the gross amount. Any tax due on those dividends is not payable until 31st January the following tax year.

INTEREST

Loan interest is *another way of extracting funds from your company.*

If you have lent your company money – perhaps to fund a deposit needed to buy the first property – then you can charge your company interest.

The interest can be at a commercial rate. This can be quite high, which is justifiable when the loan you provided was unsecured. This is likely to be the case because any lender wouldn't allow a director to have a loan secured on the property ahead of their own call on the asset.

There are three benefits to charging interest:

1. no national insurance is due on interest paid
2. company can claim a deduction for interest paid
3. every individual has a tax-free allowance of up to £1,000 for interest received (£500 for higher rate taxpayer)

There is a process to follow to pay interest from a company to an individual e.g. withholding basic rate tax and filing quarterly returns.

It's beneficial to charge some interest on a loan to the company to make full use of tax-free allowances. Husband and wife / civil partner allowances can be doubled up here for maximum benefit.

FURTHER TAX-EFFICIENT STRATEGIES TO EXTRACT CASH

You can also be tax-efficient by considering who are the company's shareholders. The company is its own legal entity and it's therefore the shareholders who can receive income and capital. The more shareholders there are, the more income can be divided between multiple tax allowances.

Anyone over 18 can hold shares in a company. (For under-18s a trust arrangement can be considered – see Chapter 11 for more).

If shares are issued at incorporation no immediate tax charges apply. This is not so for an existing property investment company that is already trading and owns a portfolio. In this case, if the company's shares have value, then any gift or new issues of shares to a connected at under-value, would give rise to a tax charge.

"The more shareholders there are, the more income can be divided between multiple tax allowances."

Further planning such as *separate classes of shares should be considered*, the benefit of such being flexibility around the quantum of dividends that can be paid up to each shareholder.

It's worth thinking carefully about how new shareholders are introduced. This is often easiest to do at the time of incorporation.

You may also want to consider having separate classes of shares. This can give the company more flexibility in the dividends that each shareholder can receive.

For example, if you just have standard ordinary shares split 40:30:30 between three people then any dividends paid up need to be in that proportion.

This is not always efficient if one individual has a greater proportion of their tax-free or basic rate threshold to use. By having different classes of shares, dividends can be voted up flexibly to suit the tax position of the individual shareholders.

Further planning can also be done on incorporation to maximise allowances within the family, e.g. using children's allowances which can be worth up to £14,500 per year for each child. This is a more advanced area of planning and advice should be taken on how this can be done to best effect according to your circumstances.

SUMMARY

There are many good reasons why the company route is the most efficient structure to grow and hold your property portfolio depending on your objectives.

Do ensure you talk to your advisor about your objectives so he or she can guide you towards the best structure that suits your needs.

Chapter 4
Can I transfer properties already owned into a company?

So far, we have looked at how to structure buying new properties given recent tax changes.

However, what's the most tax efficient route if you already have a sizeable property portfolio in your own name or held in a partnership with your spouse or other partners?

SHOULD I TRANSFER PROPERTIES I ALREADY OWN INTO A COMPANY?

This is a common question from buy-to-let landlords who hold property personally or in partnership.

Surprisingly the answer is... it depends (again!)

The default position is that any transfer of properties from one person to another gives rise to:

1. Stamp duty (plus 3% surcharge)

2. Capital gains tax due on the difference between current market value and what you paid for the property

If a transfer is between 'connected parties' in tax speak – in other words any person or company connected to you, the transfer must be undertaken at 'market value' – regardless of whether money actually changes hands for the properties.

In other words, any transfer of properties you own personally would be deemed to transfer at their market value into any company in which you own the shares – and therefore be subject to capital gains tax.

The rate of capital gains tax on residential properties is currently 28% for a higher-rate taxpayer. If you have owned properties for a while and they have increased in value then the CGT bill will probably be quite high.

WHAT CAN I DO?

In previous chapters we've seen that the tax bill for landlords who hold property personally or in partnership is likely to rocket for two main reasons:

1. Withdrawal of wear and tear allowance
2. Removal of mortgage interest relief

Number one above applies to companies too so there's not much to be done there.

Number two doesn't apply to companies and therefore for geared portfolios, i.e. if you have a reasonable amount of debt, then holding properties through a company is more tax advantageous because companies still get full tax relief for interest paid.

SPECIAL RELIEF – ADVANCED TAX PLANNING

If you meet certain criteria there may be a route for you to transfer your existing portfolio into a company FREE of CAPITAL GAINS TAX and STAMP DUTY.

There is relief within the tax legislation that allows for *trading businesses* to be transferred to a company without immediately triggering a capital gains tax charge – instead the tax charge is *deferred* until the company's shares are sold.

This relief (known as *incorporation relief*) is typically used by sole-trader businesses who transfer their businesses to a limited company as they grow. You will recall that a transfer of business or property between connected parties must take place at market value for tax purposes – even if no money changes hands. Transferring a business from one person to their own company would fall under this same rule.

To determine the amount of tax payable, a valuation of the business is normally undertaken. This is a subjective area and should be undertaken by a professional to withstand HMRC scrutiny.

However, the tax due on the value transferred can be deferred into the future providing (by and large):

- It is a *trading business* being transferred
- No cash consideration or equivalent i.e loan arrangement is made

Problem is, HMRC have always considered the act of letting property as *'investment activity'* rather than trading activity. Rental income is treated in the tax legislation and on tax returns as income from 'land and property' and as such deemed to be investment income. No national insurance is levied on rental income whereas national insurance is payable on income from a *trade* i.e business.

How can renting property be seen as a business then?

HMRC may have a view that letting out property is investment activity rather than trading activity but it doesn't mean that they are right. That is *their* interpretation of the legislation.

In reality, if you are a landlord and manage your own large portfolio as a full time property investor – and everything that comes with it – then you could argue that you are 'running a business' and therefore engaging in *trading activity*.

Recent case law and success by some landlords through the First Tier Tribunals suggests that certain activities by landlords can constitute trading activity. This is a grey area but if you can prove that you are actively managing and administering your portfolio like a business then there is scope for you to qualify for this relief.

Activities that may constitute running your property portfolio like a business include:

- undertaking viewings for potential tenants and performing tenant on-boarding process
- managing the maintenance of the portfolio
- employing staff to help administer the portfolio
- being the contact for emergency call-outs from tenants
- administering the issue and renewal of tenancy agreements
- having a business name
- finding tenants yourself via your own adverts

There is no hard and fast rule. Each case needs to be looked at on its own merits to determine if an argument can be made to HMRC that you're running a property rental business rather than being a passive property investor.

The make-up of your portfolio can also help to add weight to the argument. If you own several houses in multiple occupation (HMOs) for example, you probably deal with administrative tasks relating to individual tenants and contend with everything else involved in managing HMOs.

Perhaps running your rental business is all that you do to earn your income and you spend all your time doing so. That too helps to add weight that you are running a business and not merely a passive investor.

There is also not a certain number of properties that you need to have to meet the criteria. However, it's unlikely that you could be said to be running a business with say two or three buy-to-lets as by their nature, the properties become passive investments to supplement income from elsewhere.

However, as you start to approach ten or more properties – not a hard and fast rule but clearly more work and management is needed for that many properties – then it could be reasonably argued that the activities involved in running a portfolio of that size constitute running a business.

Notwithstanding this, you could have fewer properties but be more involved in actively managing them, for example in the case of HMOs and therefore have a case for running a property business.

Although earlier case law going back to the 1970's indicated that letting properties should be seen as investment activity, there was a fairly recent case (2013) heard in the Upper Tribunal that suggested otherwise.

The Upper Tribunal ruling in *Mrs EM Ramsay v HMRC* [2013] provides some authority for treating substantive property letting activities as a business for the purposes of s 162 incorporation relief. The tribunal ruled that activities ordinarily associated with the management of an investment property could be regarded as a business. However, to be treated in this way it held that the activities must:

- represent a seriously pursued undertaking;

- be conducted on sound and recognised business principles; and
- be of a type that is commonly made by those who seek to profit by them.

Further, the activities must be of a significant nature with a reasonable period of time being spent on property-related activities. In *Mrs EM Ramsay*, the taxpayer had devoted some 20 hours a week to managing, maintaining and carrying out property business-related work. The case also shows that it is the quantity not the quality of the activity that is important.

It clearly helps if the property owners have no other employment or trade.

BENEFIT OF INCORPORATING SUCCESSFULLY TO A COMPANY

The main benefit

If the conditions we've just looked at apply to you then you can potentially transfer your existing portfolio into a company FREE of capital gains tax. Essentially, the capital gains tax is deferred into the base cost of your shares in your new company.

This means that the capital gains tax becomes payable when you sell some, or all of, the shares in the company. What is the benefit of that approach?

The main benefit #2

In reality you will probably never sell the shares of the company. If you want to sell a property, your company which now owns it would be selling one of its properties and receiving the sale proceeds. This gives rise to another significant benefit that occurs due to the *cost of the properties as far as the company is concerned.*

The way this incorporation tax relief works is that *the properties are transferred in to the company at their market value at the time of transfer.*

This means that any 'inherent gain' i.e. *any increase in value since you bought the properties is essentially wiped out*. Of course, it isn't completely as the gain is built into the base cost of the shares but that is the clever part of the planning as you are unlikely to ever sell the shares of the new company.

You would sell the individual properties instead, in which case *you only pay tax on the difference between the amount you receive less the amount at which it transferred to the company* – say today's market value.

For portfolios held for many years and that have huge in-built gains because of the low purchase cost and the increase in property prices since, this strategy can generate substantial savings.

Example

Say, you own 10 properties that you bought for £100,000 each 10 years ago. They are each worth £200,000 now.

The default position is that you have a gain of £1 million that you would need to pay tax on at 28% i.e. £280,000 in order to transfer the portfolio to a company.

Let's say you meet the criteria needed to make a claim for the tax relief to transfer your properties to the company tax free.

The properties transfer to the company at their market value today i.e. £200,000 each. You don't pay any capital gains tax on the transfer thereby deferring the 28% of £1,000,000 i.e. £280,000.

If you then sell the properties a year later for the same amount, the company would not pay any tax at all as there has not been any increase in value from the time the company held them.

If there has been any gain in the property since the transfer, the company would pay corporation tax on the gain at company rates. These rates are due to fall to just 17% by April 2020.

Clearly a sensible approach is needed as to the timing of the sales. It should not be the intention to sell as soon as the transfer has completed. However, and as we have seen, the future sales of the properties will be subject only to tax on any gains from the date of transfer.

It's all too good to be true..

You may be thinking that these potential savings are too good to be true.

Yes, the savings are there to be had using a relief in the tax legislation that has been around for many decades. Moreover, using the relief in this way cannot be said to constitute aggressive tax planning despite the potential savings that can be achieved.

The only potential slight downside is that the proceeds from property sales come into the company. The company is a separate legal entity to its owners and therefore you need to pay some tax to extract cash from the company i.e. most commonly by dividend or salary.

However, this additional income tax can be kept to a minimum because you can:

- be flexible in the ownership structure of the company i.e. by having multiple shareholders
- choose when to take cash out from the company.

If you really wanted to extract the cash from the company in one go after selling the whole portfolio, there is another benefit to take advantage of.

Ordinarily any capital gains arising from the sale of residential property are subject to higher rates of capital gains tax of either 18% for basic rate taxpayers or 28% for higher-rate taxpayers.

In contrast, capital gains arising on the sale of any other asset are taxed at lower rates of just 20%.

Therefore, if you wanted to extract the cash funds in full in one go, you could wind up the company and receive a final distribution as a shareholder.

As the winding up involves giving up or 'selling' your shares in the company, in taxation terms you are treated as having sold *shares* rather than *property*.

As the 20% rate applies to sales of company shares (unless you qualify for Entrepreneur's Relief, in which case the rate is 10%) this generates a saving of 8 percentage points compared to paying tax at the 28% rate if property is sold at a gain in your personal name.

WHAT ABOUT STAMP DUTY?

Stamp duty normally applies on the consideration paid for property – whether or not money changes hands – from one party to another. So any transfer between you personally and your company would trigger a charge to stamp duty – as your company is considered a separate legal entity.

As we discussed earlier, the transfer is deemed to take place at 'market value' because you are connected with your company whether or not money changes hands.

Given the introduction of the 3% surcharge to residential property, the stamp duty costs payable can be a stumbling block if trying to transfer a significant portfolio – even if that transfer meets the conditions of running a property rental business.

WHEN AND HOW CAN STAMP DUTY BE AVOIDED?

As with most things in tax, there can be a work around if you meet certain criteria.

It's possible to avoid stamp duty completely on the transfer of your properties to a company if:

- you run your property business in partnership with, for example, your spouse, other family members or third parties; and
- you all actively engaged in the business to some extent.

This is due to provisions in the legislation that *apply only to partnerships* incorporating to a new limited company with the same shareholding. Essentially this provision reduces the stamp duty payable if the shareholdings in the new company mirror the partnership split.

> For example, if you have run an active partnership with your spouse in a 50:50 ratio and the new company is also structured in a 50:50 equity split, then no stamp duty is due to be paid.

If the new shareholding in the company is not exactly the same but both partners have some shareholding at least, then the stamp duty calculation will still produce some saving compared to the headline amount due.

Three factors are important here to demonstrate a bona fide partnership arrangement:

- you have an established partnership that has been actively trading in property letting
- that partnership can be demonstrated through paperwork such as a partnership agreement and
- the partnership is registered with HMRC and submits annual partnership tax returns.

What if I just own the properties in my sole name rather than a partnership?

If your property portfolio is solely in your name then, unfortunately, relief from stamp duty for transfers from a partnership to a company is not available to you.

There are however other reliefs that could help mitigate the amount of stamp duty payable. This may still make it worthwhile to consider moving your property portfolio to a company for the other capital gains and income tax benefits. (See Chapter 8 for more details.)

Alternatively, it may be possible to start a partnership with a view perhaps to use the above relief in the future.

In this case, a partnership with your spouse would make the most sense because an introduction of any other partner you would have to pay capital-gains tax on the sale of your share in the portfolio to this other person.

Next steps

If you think you might meet the above criteria to avoid both capital gains tax and stamp duty, it is worth taking advice as soon as possible to check on this.

We have helped several landlords with large portfolios successfully incorporate their property holdings without their having to pay capital gains or stamp duty.

Case Study

Mr and Mrs S owned a large portfolio of student and professional accommodation valued at about £20 million. They had interest payments of about £250,000 on a loan of approximately £9 million.

As they were trading in partnership, the withdrawal of interest relief meant that by 2020 their annual tax bills would increase by £100,000 i.e. 40% x £250,000.

We explored the incorporation route and deemed that we could put a strong case together to HMRC for them to claim the capital gains tax and stamp duty reliefs.

We helped them to complete the transfer of the properties to the company and to refinance the debt in the name of the new company.

They saved £2.4 million in capital gains tax and £1.3 million in stamp duty.

They were very happy!

If you'd like to discuss whether you could benefit from similar planning, feel free to get in touch.

"We have helped several landlords with large portfolios successfully incorporate their property holdings without their having to pay capital gains or stamp duty."

Chapter 5

Do I have to worry about VAT on property?

Normally, if you are only involved in letting residential property then you do not need to worry about VAT. Letting property is an 'exempt supply' for VAT purposes; this means that you do not charge VAT on the rent nor can you recover any VAT paid for expenses incurred in managing your rental business.

However, there are circumstances when property and VAT do mix. This is typically when you are involved in one or more of the following:

- buying / renting commercial property
- developing / converting commercial property to residential property, or
- building new residential property.

BUYING / RENTING COMMERCIAL PROPERTY

When buying commercial property there may be VAT considerations. You will most likely be faced with one of the following situations:

1. buying a property with VAT
2. buying a property without VAT

Although the general rule with property is that it is VAT exempt, it is possible to waive this exemption and make the property 'VAT-able'. This is also known as 'opting to tax' the property.

When a property is opted it means that any supplies made from it are subject to VAT i.e. rents needs to have VAT added; also if the property is sold then VAT will be added to the purchase price.

This strategy can be quite beneficial.

Take the example of a typical commercial tenant: a retail store.

As a landlord you need to charge VAT on the rent. That would not be a problem for the retail store as they are likely to be VAT registered and can therefore reclaim the VAT.

So it is not a cost to their business (except, it could be argued, having a small impact on their cashflow).

The landlord can recover VAT on all costs associated with letting the property to the commercial tenant e.g. repairs, building works, professional fees etc.

More importantly if as the landlord you intend to make 'taxable supplies' from the property then you can *reclaim the VAT paid on the purchase price.*

There can be times when opting to tax a property may not be beneficial.

If your tenant is a dentist for example. Healthcare services are generally VAT exempt, so the dentist cannot recover the VAT paid on rent. This added cost makes the lease less attractive to a dental practice compared to a VAT-registered business.

Properties are opted on a building by building basis so you could own several commercial properties within a company but only choose to opt the ones that are beneficial to do so. It is the property that is opted rather than the entity or individual that owns the property.

When buying commercial property make sure you take advice on whether to opt or not depending both on your current circumstances and your plans for the property.

TRANSFER OF GOING CONCERN

A useful technique to avoid paying VAT on a VAT-registered property is making use of the Transfer of Going Concern (TOGC) rules. Providing you meet certain criteria as wet out below, you can avoid paying VAT to the seller and thereby reduce the cashflow needed to complete the purchase.

This can be particularly beneficial if you need to take out a mortgage on the purchase as it reduces the amount you need to borrow.

These, broadly, are the conditions:

- property must currently be let to a tenant
- both the buyer and seller must be VAT-registered at time of exchange
- buyer must opt to tax the property
- transfer documents should be for 'transfer of a letting business'

The VAT rules recognise property letting as a business activity. So the transfer of a property being let under a lease to another person can be considered as a transfer of a business under the VAT legislation.

If you find you meet the above criteria then it's worth talking to your accountants and solicitors about structuring the purchase as a TOGC to avoid paying VAT on the purchase.

Save on stamp duty

An added advantage of a transfer done as a TOGC? *You pay less stamp duty.* Stamp duty is on the VAT-inclusive cost of a property.

If VAT is payable on a purchase then stamp duty on the VAT is added to the total stamp duty payable. If there is no VAT payable then stamp duty is reduced accordingly.

CONVERSION OF COMMERCIAL PROPERTIES TO RESIDENTIAL

Given the stark housing shortage in the UK, the conversion of properties from commercial to residential has been commonplace across many cities. From pubs, high street offices, closed-down care homes and even industrial buildings, they have all seen a change of use from commercial to residential apartments.

The reduced rate

As we've just seen, the default position for letting residential property is that it is exempt. That means any VAT incurred on costs is not normally recoverable.

What about when you buy a commercial property and want to convert it to residential use?

There is a reduced rate of VAT of 5% that applies for conversion to residential use. If you are not VAT-registered then this limits the amount of VAT that can be charged to you to 5% as opposed to 20% – a helpful reduction.

You need to certify to your suppliers that you are carrying out conversion works to ensure that they reduce the VAT charged on your invoices to 5%.

"When buying commercial property there may be VAT considerations."

Can I reclaim this 5% too?

As we've seen you can opt to make a property 'VAT-able' and thereby recover VAT paid on purchase or other costs incurred. However, the principle condition attached to this ability to opt is that you must intend to make 'taxable supplies' from the property.

As explained at the start of this chapter, letting property is an exempt supply as far as VAT is concerned. So if you plan to let the properties after converting them then that is not a 'taxable activity' and you cannot reclaim the VAT on the conversion works.

If on the other hand you intend to sell the properties after conversion, that does constitute a 'taxable supply' because the first sale of a new residential dwelling qualifies as a taxable supply.

Advanced tip

You can however recover the VAT paid on the property purchase and the conversion works without having to sell the properties.

This is an advanced area of VAT planning that involves granting a long lease on the residential flats to another company.

The grant of a long lease is a 'taxable supply' and means that you qualify for that main condition of making 'taxable supplies' from the property. You can therefore reclaim the VAT paid in full.

If you find yourself in this situation, take advice as careful planning could save you thousands of pounds in VAT costs.

In the next chapter we will look at the VAT implications of property development.

Chapter 6

How should I structure property development activities?

WHAT IS 'PROPERTY DEVELOPMENT'?

The definition of property development is quite wide. A practical definition is something along these lines:

"the act of buying a property or land, doing something to it i.e. converting, renovating or building something and then selling it with a view to making a profit"

If what you are buying meets the above definition then you are most likely engaged in property development.

DOES IT MATTER?

For tax purposes, yes. In tax terms, property investment (buying something to rent out) is taxed differently from property development. HMRC considers the former as *investment activity* (by default) and the latter as *trading activity*.

So how is property development taxed?

As HMRC considers this activity as *trading activity*, it's subject to the same tax treatment as if you're running a business. In general any profits from property development incur income tax if you are a sole trader or in partnership and liable to corporation tax if conducted via a company.

Properties or land purchased are classified as *trading stock* in your accounts as opposed to *fixed assets* or *investments*. In this sense you buy the stock, spend money to improve it then sell the stock which appears in your profit and loss account – as a profit or loss.

The difference with *property investment* is that the sale of investment property (when held personally or in partnership) is subject to capital gains taxes which are different to income tax.

For a long time now, capital gains taxes have been much lower than the highest rate of income tax. At present the highest rate of capital gains tax is 28% compared to 45% for income tax. In addition there is a separate annual allowance for capital gains of £12,000 (currently) each which helps to reduce the tax payable.

For companies however, there is no difference in the tax rate when selling a capital asset. The 'capital gain' that results when a profit on sale in made is subject to corporation tax – same as the 'income' earned from the properties.

WHAT STRUCTURE SHOULD I USE FOR PROPERTY DEVELOPMENT?

If you are engaged in property development you might fall within one of these two camps:

1. Self-developer – you run your own business buying up plots of land or properties where you can add value and sell at a profit. You

engage and direct the respective trades to do the necessary. You may be a builder by background.

2. Property developer – you source the sites where you believe a profit can be made, source the finance (either self, bank or investor) and then manage the development with respective trades or a main contractor to complete the project.

The structure you adopt depends on which of the above camps you fall into.

If you are a self-developer, you probably already have a trading company that buys the sites – treated as stock – and you then get planning, carry out works and sell at a profit. It's likely that you use the same company to carry out all your property development.

For the property developer

If you fall into the second camp, you may need to have separate entities (SPV's) depending on your objectives *for* each development and how each development is funded.

Funders are more likely to lend to an SPV where the company's activity can be limited to real estate developments only.

In expansion / growth phase

When starting out and sourcing your first deals, you probably need to put in a reasonable amount of your own cash to persuade a third-party funder to support your development.

Once you have a track record then you should be able to borrow at better rates and have more funding options available.

At that stage therefore, *the most appropriate structure is probably a limited company*. You can limit the exposure to the assets of the limited company (unless the bank insists upon personal guarantees) and *start to build up profits for reinvestment*.

Attracting investors phase

Once you have successfully undertaken projects and delivered a profit, you may find that others want you to do the same for them. They are prepared to put in the money for you to invest in a property deal and share the profits with you.

In this case you may want to structure it through what is known in the industry as an 'SPV'.

WHAT IS AN SPV?

The term SPV stands for 'Special Purpose Vehicle'. In essence it is just an alternative term for a legal entity within which a business is run, or an investment held, i.e. a limited company or limited liability partnership (LLP).

SPVs are commonly used for property development deals as it enables that project to be ringfenced and set up with the stakeholders for that deal.

As a developer you may work with different investors and lenders on a project. An SPV means that every stakeholder's interests can be protected and risks mitigated. What's more any charge or security taken by a lender is restricted to the asset held by the SPV.

In fact, some lenders are quite particular and require the SIC code of the SPV to fall into a specific real estate category. The SIC code stands for 'Standard Industrial Classification' code and is used to provide a description of a company's activities at the time of registration. This SIC code is then publicly available via Companies House and serve as an indicator of what the company is set up to do.

There are commercial reasons therefore for property development to be structured via an SPV.

Ltd or LLP

Given that property development is seen as 'trading activity' from a tax perspective, it's normally better for an SPV to be structured as a limited company than as an LLP.

This is mainly because an LLP is *'see through'* for tax purposes, meaning that it does not account for tax on profits in its own right. Instead each partner of the LLP is attributed their share of profit, which is then subject to income tax – where the partner is an individual.

Each partner is potentially subject to the highest rate of income tax on some of the profits earned. That rate is currently 45%. National insurance of 2% on profits above the basic rate limit also applies.

In contrast, the limited company is a *'taxable person'* in its own right and therefore pays corporation tax on profits earned from the sale of a development. Corporation tax is currently 19% and due to fall to 17% by 2020.

Thereafter the profit left after corporation tax paid is available to the company's shareholders to withdraw should they wish to. Extracting this profit can be done in one of two ways:

1. by dividend
2. by a capital distribution

Extracting profits by dividend

Drawing the profits left by way of dividend is relatively self-explanatory and straightforward. Shareholders are subject to their marginal rates of income tax on any dividends. The rates of income tax on dividends are currently 32.5% for a higher-rate tax payer and 38.1% for a top-rate taxpayer i.e. income over £150,000.

Remember however that dividends can be spread across a number of years and also between shareholders. So think about who else you can bring on board as shareholders at the outset to share the profits out tax-efficiently at the end.

Extracting profits by Capital Distribution

The other way of extracting the company's remaining profit is a *capital distribution*. Shareholders need to sell the shares of the company, which is treated as a disposal of an asset by an individual and therefore subject to capital gains tax.

It's unlikely you can sell your shares in the company to anyone else for its value because the company only has the cash left over from sale of the development.

You can put the company into *'voluntary liquidation'* to achieve the same effect for tax purposes. This might sound drastic but is a perfectly normal way of winding up a company and for the shareholders to get their share of the profit left in the company.

A distribution received by a shareholder once the company is liquidated is always treated as a *'capital distribution'*.

Only a licensed insolvency practitioner can undertake the practical aspects of a *voluntary liquidation*. However this should be relatively straightforward if the only thing left in the company is the cash proceeds from the sale of the development.

All liabilities must be settled before the insolvency practitioner is appointed. Otherwise creditors could block the liquidation if they are still owed money and they become aware that the company is about to be wound up.

Typically the main creditors would be the Crown i.e. HMRC for any taxes due and possibly any trade creditors. Do ensure that everyone is paid before starting this process.

When you receive a capital distribution, your gain for tax purposes is the difference between what you acquired the shares for (typically nominal value i.e. £100) and the amount you receive on the capital distribution i.e. your share of the profit.

This amount is then subject to *capital gains tax*.

This allows you to fall within the capital gains tax regime *which has lower tax rates than income tax* rates on dividends.

Of course, there are extra costs involved in a voluntary liquidation by having to appoint a licensed insolvency practitioner. However the amount saved in tax by falling within capital gains treatment should more than offset this cost.

So what is the tax payable on a capital distribution?

Ordinarily a sale of shares (which is essentially how a capital distribution is treated) results in capital gains tax on the profit at 20% unless you qualify for *Entrepreneur's Relief*.

Entrepreneur's Relief is available when you sell shares in a *trading company*. Given that property development is considered a trading activity, you can potentially claim this relief and therefore reduce your tax on the gain to just 10%.

This is a substantial saving and *reduces the overall effective rate of tax to less than 27%* compared to nearly 50% on the dividend route.

Example

You carry out a property deal and make a profit of £1 million after all expenses but before corporation tax. This table shows the overall taxes paid to get all the cash from the profit into your hands – comparing both the routes described above i.e. by dividend or capital distribution. Assumption has been made that you want access to all the cash immediately. Obviously you could draw smaller dividends over a longer period of time that might help to reduce the tax payable on dividends.

	Dividend route	**Capital distribution route**
Profit before tax	£1,000,000	£1,000,000
Corporation tax @19%	(£190,000)	(£190,000)
Profit after tax available for distribution to shareholders	£810,000	£810,000
Income tax @ 38.1%	(£308,610)	
Capital gains tax @ 10%		(£81,000)
Cash in hand upon extraction	£501,390	£729,000
Effective rate of total taxes paid	**50%**	**27%**

As you can see, there is massive differential between extracting the profits by dividend or by capital distribution with the effective rates of tax being 50% and 27% respectively.

Overall there is a tax saving of up to 23 percentage points on the amount of profit made.

Bear in mind there are other criteria to qualify for Entrepreneur's Relief, most notably:

- be an *employee or director* of the company

- have at least a 5% shareholding (with rights to capital and dividends) and
- hold the shares for at least *2 years* (change effective from April 2019).

That condition of a two-year holding may prove problematic for some short-term developments.

If you buy something, renovate it and sell it in less than two years, you cannot wind up the company and take out a capital distribution that falls within Entrepreneur's Relief as you would not have held the shares for two years.

In that case if the cash is needed then the company can still be wound up and a capital distribution taken. However the tax on the distribution would be 20% rather than 10% – still better than taking the profits via dividends.

"In tax terms, property investment (buying something to rent out) is taxed differently from property development."

What to watch out for

Furthermore, anti-avoidance legislation was introduced in 2016 to clamp down on people who were 'phoenixing' companies and claiming Entrepreneur's Relief.

This new legislation was designed to prevent individuals accumulating profit in a company, then winding it up to extract the funds at 10% before starting up the same trade in a new company and repeating the process after a couple of years.

The legislation now prevents claiming Entrepreneur's Relief if the individual starts a similar business within two years of closing the previous one.

As the legislation is quite new, it hasn't been tested on property developers yet as this would catch a large majority of them. However, the difference between property developers and the individuals that the legislation was designed to catch is, that property developers set up the structure in this way primarily for commercial reasons rather than for tax purposes.

We mentioned earlier that the main reason for setting up the SPV is so that assets can be ringfenced and liabilities limited to the specific project.

It's therefore difficult to see how HMRC could see this as the same arrangements as those engaged in 'phoenixing'. However based on how the legislation has been drafted, there is no exception made for property developers.

If Entrepreneur's Relief is not available then under the worst-case scenario the profit extracted after corporation tax is taxed at the 20% rate of capital gains tax rather than 10%. This is still better than going down the LLP or dividend route if you plan to extract the funds in one go.

NEW BUILDS AND VAT

If you are a developer or engaging a developer to build a new residential or commercial property then the first sale of that property would fall within the zero-rating VAT rules.

This means that no VAT is chargeable to the buyer. However as the first sale of the property qualifies for 'zero rating' it qualifies as a 'taxable supply' so any VAT incurred on the build can be reclaimed in full.

To qualify as a new build and to meet the definition of a 'relevant residential purpose' these conditions must be met:

- home or institution providing residential care for children, elderly, hospice; or
- residential accommodation for students
- monastery, nunnery or similar establishment

Zero rating also applies where the conditions for a 'relevant charitable purpose' are met. Broadly where a building is being constructed for use by a charity for their own charitable purposes (rather than for letting).

Is anything not included?

Zero rating does not apply to the services of an architect, surveyor, consultant or any other person acting in a supervisory capacity. These costs will be standard rated.

Building materials can be zero rated if supplied with the labour provided by the sub-contractor. However if building materials are bought separately then they will always be standard rated i.e. at 20%.

DIY HOUSEBUILDERS AND VAT

A special refund scheme puts DIY housebuilders and converters in a similar position to a developer selling them a zero-rated property. This means if you are building your own home from scratch or converting a non residential building into dwelling, you can potentially recover VAT on the main construction or major conversion costs if you meet certain criteria.

If this is something that you are involved in, then do take advice as it could save you a lot of money by not having to pay VAT.

Chapter 7

What records do I need to keep for my property portfolio?

The key to being able to mitigate taxes is having up-to-date, real-time information in the first place.

From this information you / your tax advisor should be able to project your tax position for the year and suggest any measures to reduce your tax bill in good time.

It's also good practice to have up-to-date records to help you monitor your property portfolio's performance and see the return on investment that it's generating.

WHAT'S THE BEST WAY TO MAINTAIN MY RECORDS?

With cloud accounting software, it's now easier than ever to keep your property rental accounts up-to-date. Software such as Quickbooks Online and Xero allow bank transactions to be pulled into the software automatically so that your accounts are kept updated.

Furthermore, as the software is cloud based, you can collaborate better with your accountant, who can log in to the software at any time to review the figures or help to keep reconciliations up-to-date.

Over and above the tax advantages of real-time information, you should also configure your chosen software package to give you more insightful management information on your rental portfolio.

Meaningful insights like these can be generated:

- rental profit by property
- return on investment by property and across the whole portfolio
- gearing ratio i.e. level of debt as a percentage of the portfolio value
- gross and net rental yields

Choosing key metrics such as these to monitor and track will keep you focused on running an efficient and profitable real-estate portfolio.

OTHER ADVANTAGES OF REAL-TIME INFORMATION

If you plan to expand your portfolio and earn the greatest return from your real-estate investments, you will probably want to leverage your portfolio at some point.

Lending criteria have become a lot stricter since the credit crunch and lenders are increasingly selective about who gets the best deals. They favour investors with a track record rather than new entrants to the market.

You can increase your credibility with any financier by the quality and timeliness of your management information.

Giving the lender up-to-date management accounts on your portfolio, profit and loss reports by property, gearing ratio calculations etc. will go a long way to establish yourself as a credible recipient of funding in the eyes of any credit committee.

The *speed at which you can get a lender the information requested also makes a difference*. Reports can be generated quite easily and quickly if your financials are kept up-to-date within accounting software.

Being able to pull off this information and having it with you in that first meeting with a lender will make a massive difference in how you are perceived – and greatly increase your chances of getting favourable funding offers.

To add further credibility, have your accountant review and send these to the bank and boost your chances of getting the best deal. Inevitably the lender will need your accountant on board to verify and certify the figures to provide the mortgage references needed to complete the credit application.

"You can increase your credibility with any financier by the quality and timeliness of your management information."

Making Tax Digital

HMRC launched their Making Tax Digital initiative which requires VAT registered businesses to submit their quarterly information via approved third party software. This has led to thousands of businesses that were not already maintaining their accounting records via any software to promptly digitise their records.

MTD kicked in from April 2019. HMRC initially had announced that it would apply to landlords with over £10,000 income (that's total rents, not profit) too. However they subsequently backtracked and postponed *the obligation for landlords until April 2020.*

In any case, from April 2020 most landlords (let's face it, even if you have one flat that is renting out at £900/month then you would be caught) will need to digitally provide information to HMRC every quarter.

This information will need to include details of income and expenditure of the property business. Total income and expenditure for the whole property business will be sufficient (rather than split by property) although they will need you to send the property information details eg. Address etc.

In summary the data required by HMRC is the following:

- rental amount
- invoice date and expense amount
- expense category (to match tax return)
- any disallowed percentage for personal use (for properties in personal name)

If you're not already doing so, then time has come for you to get your records maintained on cloud software. Although HMRC have made some tweaks to potentially allow submissions via Excel spreadsheets, these are not terribly efficient at maintaining proper reconciled records when compared to cloud accounting software.

Will I have to pay tax quarterly?

HMRC have not changed when the tax is due to be paid although one can not rule this out for the future. The quarterly returns will require submission one month after the quarter end – similar to VAT return reporting.

Is this yet another compliance burden on the small business?

It is a pain having to confirm to another compliance burden introduced by HMRC however in my opinion this is a blessing. The power of up to date management information is so much more beneficial to you in running your property business so it's something you should be doing anyway.

It is then no additional headache to supply HMRC with something that you are already doing yourself to run a better, more efficient and dynamic property business.

Furthermore, how many expenses have been missed because you lost the receipt, paid by cash or forgot about it when it came to doing your end of year tax return one year later? Having to keep updated information via accounting software linked to your bank account means that you are more likely to capture all expense and therefore *claim all the tax back that you are due*.

Chapter 8
Can I reduce the stamp duty I pay?

Following the introduction of the 3% stamp-duty surcharge, stamp duty now represents a fairly significant proportion of total purchase costs.

It's important to take into account both stamp duty and other direct costs associated with a purchase when working out the projected yield on the property to see if it represents an adequate return on investment.

Let's take a look at the stamp duty rates that apply to both residential (with surcharge) and non-residential properties below.

Buy to let / additional home rate (residential)

Purchase price of property	Rate of stamp duty	Buy to let / additional home rate
£0 – £125,000	0%	3%
£125,001 – £250,000	2%	5%
£250,001 – £925,000	5%	8%
£925,001 – £1,500,000	10%	13%
£1,500,001 –	12%	15%

The stamp duty is worked out on increasing portions of the property price over £125,000 so a buy o let property bought at £300,000, the SDLT would be [(£125,000 x 3%) + (£125,000 x 5%) + (£50,000 x 8%)] = £14,000

Non-residential rate / commercial property

Purchase price of property	Rate of stamp duty
£0 – £150,000	0%
£150,001 – £250,000	2%
Over £250,001	5%

The stamp duty for non residential properties is also worked out on increasing portions so a purchase of a commercial property for £300,000 would give rise to stamp duty of the following:

[£150,000 x 0% + £100,000 x 2% + £50,000 x 5%] = £4,500

Clearly the stamp duty regime is a lot more favourable to investment into commercial properties than residential properties.

IS THERE ANY WAY TO REDUCE STAMP DUTY?

Unfortunately stamp duty is quite a rigid tax in that there are not many ways it can be avoided. Aggressive schemes developed in the past by avoidance promoters have all been shut down and attacked by HMRC.

However there are some little-known options that can reduce stamp duty in certain circumstances.

Mixed-use properties

Where a property has both residential and non-residential uses, the non-residential rates of stamp duty apply. There is no apportionment either so this can represent a sizeable saving from the ordinary stamp duty rates that would apply to residential property.

The 3% surcharge does not apply to non-residential property so that would be a further saving. Typical examples include buying a ground-floor commercial unit with flats above.

Multiple purchases

If six or more residential units are purchased or transferred as part of a single transaction then the non-residential rates of stamp duty should apply to the total price.

Again this can be quite beneficial particularly if you are transferring properties from personal ownership to a limited company.

Multiple Dwellings Relief

Finally when two or more properties are purchased or transferred as part of a single transaction it may be possible to claim for Multiple Dwellings Relief (MDR).

The relief calculates the amount of stamp duty payable (subject to the surcharge rates) based on the average value of the properties transferred. If six or more properties are transferred, it's worth calculating whether it's beneficial either:

- to treat the properties as non-residential and pay the generally lower non-residential rates of stamp duty on a higher aggregate purchase price, or
- to claim MDR and pay the generally higher surcharge rates of stamp duty, but on a lower average purchase price.

The total purchase price paid for multiple properties can be divided by the number of dwellings. Then you can apply the stamp-duty rate that applies for the value by dwelling – rather than on the total purchase cost.

Example

Let's say you have six buy-to-let properties. You wish to transfer them to a limited company and the total value of the properties is £1,500,000.

Ordinarily, a transfer of residential property valued at £1,500,000 from an individual to a connected company would incur stamp duty of £138,750.

However, as six properties are transferred as part of a single transaction, we can apply the lower non-residential rates so the stamp duty becomes just £64,500 – less than half the above amount.

If a claim for MDR bis made instead, stamp duty is calculated on the average price of the properties transferred i.e. £250,000, which would produce a charge of only £60,000.

It would be beneficial to make a claim for MDR as the total saving is nearly £80,000.

Let's look at another associated example:

If we take the above example, but increase the aggregate property value to £2,500,000, the total amount of stamp duty due if the properties are deemed as non-residential is £114,500.

However, if a claim for MDR is made, the stamp duty charge is £139,998.

In this instance, it's better to deem the properties to be non-residential. This highlights the effect of the surcharge rates of stamp duty on higher-value residential properties.

This is a very valuable relief that can be claimed where you are buying more than one property at the same time as part of the same purchase.

"There are some little-known options that can reduce stamp duty in certain circumstances."

Do take advice on this if you think you could fall within it as the possible savings can be substantial. Don't assume that your solicitor will automatically do this for you!

It's important to take specialist advice at an early stage to avoid paying too much tax.

Chapter 9
Can I hold property via a pension?

Traditional pensions have got a bad press over the years – and perhaps rightly so. That's mainly because the underlying investments of pensions are outside our control and in the hands of large insurance companies or fund managers.

However there's a type of pension that may appeal more to entrepreneurs and/or property investors that gives full control over the underlying investments held in a pension scheme whilst still allowing for all the tax advantages afforded to pensions.

You may have heard of a SIPP or Self Invested Personal Pension that gives some element of control.

A SIPP can be set up with most investment managers. It allows you to choose which funds you want to hold in your pension. A SIPP can also hold commercial property; however given the nature of SIPPs, an independent trustee also sits with you on the SIPP board. That means all decisions must be taken with their consent.

WHAT IS A SSAS PENSION SCHEME?

A less well-known pension vehicle that affords much more flexibility and control is called a SSAS, or Small Self Administered Scheme, which can be set up as a company-sponsored scheme.

Typically the Trustees of a SSAS are Directors of the company and use the SSAS to make pension contributions on behalf of the Directors.

It's possible for only the Directors to be the Trustees of the scheme and, providing the Directors are 'fit and proper' and know when to take advice about the investments held by the SSAS, then this is acceptable.

For added peace of mind and comfort, there is also the option to have a SSAS Trustee company acting as co-Trustee of the SSAS with the Directors. The company's role is to make sure that:

- all investments made by the Trustees are in line with the pensions legislation (so that the tax relief claimed is not jeopardised) and
- transactions between 'connected parties', e.g. between the Trustees and the company, all take place at arm's length.

For example, if the SSAS is buying a property from the company you have a situation in which the buyer (Trustees of the SSAS) and the seller (Directors of the company) are essentially the same people.

In this case it may be tempting to take shortcuts in the legal process given that both buyer and seller are the same. However, it's important that transactions between connected parties happen as if the parties were not connected.

In the case of a property sale, proper searches should be carried out, an Energy Performance Certificate obtained, a valuation arranged, and a solicitor appointed to do the conveyancing among any other steps that would normally be taken in such a transaction.

"There's a type of pension that may appeal more to entrepreneurs and/or property investors."

HOW MUCH CAN BE INVESTED INTO A PENSION?

Currently the annual pension allowances are quite generous, allowing a contribution of up to £40,000 a year on behalf of each director, providing the director's total annual income is less than £150,000.

It's also possible to make contributions covering the previous three years if those allowances haven't been used. Therefore if no allowances have been used in earlier years, a potential £160,000 contribution could be made for one director alone.

WHAT CAN THE PENSION INVEST IN?

The rules governing the investments that pensions are allowed to make are quite strict but, broadly speaking, so long as it's not residential property or anything that's dubious from an investment perspective then it may qualify.

Holding commercial property is the most common use of a SSAS, and more often than not, the trading property from which a business operates. This provides the following advantages:

- Protected entity for the property in case of claims made against the trading company
- Rents are received tax free in the pension to accumulate a fund for the Directors' pensions
- Rents are tax deductible for the trading company

The first point is a compelling enough reason to create a SSAS to hold a business' trading property because it separates out the bricks-and-mortar safer investment from the inherently risky nature of any trading business.

SO HOW DO WE GET THE PROPERTY INTO A SSAS?

There are two main ways for a SSAS to buy a commercial property:

a) SSAS is funded by company with cash and / or mortgage to purchase property

b) SSAS receives pension cash from other pension schemes to facilitate purchase

A combination of both a) and b) is feasible too.

Generally we see the following scenarios:

- Company already owns the property from which the business trades

This is a common occurrence if the trading company has already bought the property because that's where the cash was and / or the bank was willing to lend handsomely against the property to facilitate the purchase.

Some years down the line, the mortgage may have been paid off or significantly reduced. At that point the directors are keen to separate out the investment property from the trading business. There may also be surplus cash in the business available for the Directors to extract.

In this scenario, a SSAS can be set up and funded by contributions from the company to buy the property from the company. The transaction must be at market value as the SSAS will be considered to be connected with the trading company (because the individuals are the same on each side of the transaction).

The main benefit here is that contributions made into the SSAS should qualify for corporation tax relief. It's possible to get large sums into the SSAS, which can cut the corporation tax bill significantly.

As we have seen, the company can potentially contribute £160,000 for each director providing all pension allowances over the three years are available. This normally allows for plenty of headroom to facilitate a transfer of the property out of the company and into the protected SSAS.

The other scenario is:

- Directors looking to buy commercial premises

If there's a property purchase on the horizon then exploring the acquisition via a SSAS could be beneficial.

Ordinarily if a commercial property is bought in individual names, the deposit needs to be found from other sources or taken out from the company. If the company buys the property then the deposit may already be available.

Even if that's the case, however, the acquisition via SSAS offers a unique advantage.

The benefit is that if the deposit or full purchase is fully funded in cash, then it's entirely tax deductible. In that case there's essentially a cash benefit equal to the corporation tax rate of the amount of cash invested – currently 19%.

Let's look at an example.

Say you have found a commercial property you are looking to buy for £300,000. Your company has enough funds to do this with cash.

You buy the property for cash and it sits on your balance sheet. There has been no profit or loss impact and therefore no change in your tax bill as a result of the purchase.

Now let's say you take the SSAS route.

You have available allowances among the directors to make contributions into the SSAS of £300,000. This would generate a tax deduction in the trading company equal to 19% x £300,000 i.e. £57,000.

The SSAS buys the property and signs a lease with the trading company to rent it out at £25,000 a year. Every year the company gets tax relief on the rent it pays; this equates to 19% x £25,000 = £4,750. The £25,000 goes into the SSAS tax-free to build up the Directors' respective pension pots.

As you can see, there are unique tax advantages afforded to registered pension schemes including self-controlled ones such as a SSAS. Therefore having a SSAS as part of your overall tax-efficient structures is beneficial.

Can a SSAS borrow?

Yes, however a SSAS (or SIPP for that matter) can only borrow only 50% of its net assets. So if you are short of funds and need to gear up heavily then perhaps the full benefits of the SSAS may not be open to you.

However, you can buy smaller shares of a property and over time build up a larger share. In other words, the SSAS can be a joint owner of the property with the company, for example, and buy shares in the property over time.

What's more, gearing up to 50% in the pension can be beneficial because the rents received in return go towards paying off the debt a lot faster. As *pensions don't pay income tax on any rents received then all the rent can be used to repay the debt.*

Can I transfer monies from existing pensions?

Yes, you can. It's also very useful to pool cash and consolidate all pensions in one place to facilitate a significant purchase.

All those pensions that you may have forgotten about can be valued. A notice can be sent to the provider to transfer the pension into your SSAS. Given that it's a registered pension scheme this is perfectly legitimate. There should be no issue with your pension provider agreeing to this.

Chapter 10

Advanced structures for holding property for entrepreneurs

It's not unusual for property investment to take place as a side activity from a main trading business. Entrepreneurs who have built successful businesses generate surplus profit and cash and then often look to invest into a more passive investment to diversify risk.

Property has been viewed as a safe, passive investment over the years given the returns achievable compared to other asset classes such as stock or shares – typically seen as higher risk from an entrepreneur's perspective.

In this chapter we will consider the most efficient structure if you already operate a trading company in which there's spare cash available to invest in property.

THE DEFAULT POSITION

Business owners often use cash sitting in their trading company to buy property. This may be commercial property for use by the business or other property for investment purposes.

This is understandable as the cash is already in the company and is easy to deploy for that purpose.

Any other route – for example extracting the cash into personal names for investment – would incur a tax charge.

However, buying property in the company's name is not generally the best strategy – either from a tax or commercial standpoint. Here's why:

- property (a valuable asset) is exposed to creditors within the trading company should any
- in the event of needing to sell the property – either as part of selling the trading business or as a separate sale of the property owned by that business – the trading company would pay tax on:
    - any gain in the increase in value of the property and
    - getting the resulting proceeds out of the company.

"The property can then be rented to the company at market value."

ALTERNATIVE POSITIONS

Other ways of structuring a property purchase could be:

1. personal ownership
2. pension (eg SSAS or SIPP)
3. associated company i.e. another company with common shareholders
4. holding company
5. group investment subsidiary

Let's look at each of these options in turn.

Personal ownership

Buying property in your personal name (or joint names with a spouse / business partner) is a common way of holding property used in business.

The property can then be rented to the company at market value and earn a return on investment for the owners. This can be a good way of building up a pension nest.

However rental income is fully subject to income tax at your marginal rate. If you're already a higher-rate taxpayer then rental income would be subject to the 40% rate – or as a top-rate taxpayer it would be subject to tax at 45%.

The main challenge is getting the cash into personal names to buy property in this way. Taking the cash from the company will incur a tax cost.

Advantages

- outside of higher-risk trading company environment
- disposal of property only triggers one tax charge i.e. CGT (higher rate of CGT if residential property)
- cash is received in hand

Disadvantages

- rental income taxed at highest marginal rates to income tax
- rental income taxed – whether cash used or not – as tax is levied on profit made
- extraction of cash from company gives rise to tax charge

Pension ownership

As we saw in Chapter 9, holding property via a pension – preferably a SSAS – can be quite tax efficient.

It also resolves the issue of shielding valuable property from potential creditors because the pension trust is a separate legal entity from the company.

The company rents the property from the pension at market value and gets tax relief for this rent. The *pension in turn doesn't pay tax on the rent it receives.*

Moreover if there's cash in the company this can be contributed to the pension scheme as part of directors' overall remuneration, benefiting from corporation tax relief in the process.

Depending on allowances available, this essentially means that you get *19% (current corporation tax rate) of the purchase price back from HMRC in the form of a tax deduction.*

In conclusion the pros and cons of pension ownership can be summarised as follows:

Advantages

- tax relief on contributions to scheme to fund purchase
- tax relief on rents paid to pension
- tax-free rental income accruing in pension
- no capital gains payable by pension

Disadvantages

- pension can only buy commercial, not residential, property
- income accruing in pension can't be accessed until retirement age
- property can be sold by pension but cash stays in pension until retirement age

Associated company

The property can be bought by an associated company – i.e. a property under the control of common shareholders.

The initial challenge will be getting the cash into the associated company. This can be done by a loan – to avoid paying tax on extracting the cash from the company and re-injecting it – or by subscribing for shares in the company.

The latter route makes the associated company a subsidiary of the trading company. We will look at that in a later point dealing with this method.

Advantages

- keeps property separate from main trading company
- mitigates against risk of Entrepreneur's Relief not being available in trading company
- rental profits are taxed at lower corporate rates and available for reinvestment

Disadvantages

- initial injection of cash from trading company to associated company is problematic

- when the trading company is sold, loan balance created on initial transfer will need to be settled.

Holding company

It's possible to undertake a corporate restructuring to create a holding company that owns the shares in the trading company. This achieves separation of the entity holding the property from the trading entity.

Any cash available in the trading company can be transferred to the holding company (free of tax) and used to buy the property investment. The holding company can then rent the property to the trading company.

From a tax perspective, the holding company receiving the rent pays tax on the rents while the trading company receives a tax deduction for the rent paid. This makes the transaction tax neutral.

This structure is suitable if you're buying commercial property to be used in the company's day-to-day business.

The group structure would look as follows:

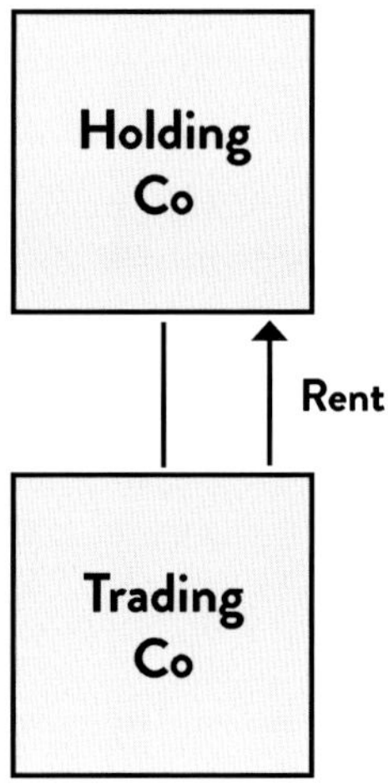

Advantages

- separation of property ownership from trading to reduce risk
- creation of group for future expansion

Disadvantages

- may hamper access to Entrepreneur's Relief because shares are no longer held directly in the trading company

Group investment subsidiary

This route is an extension of the holding company structure and involves setting up a group property investment company under a holding company. The structure is shown below:

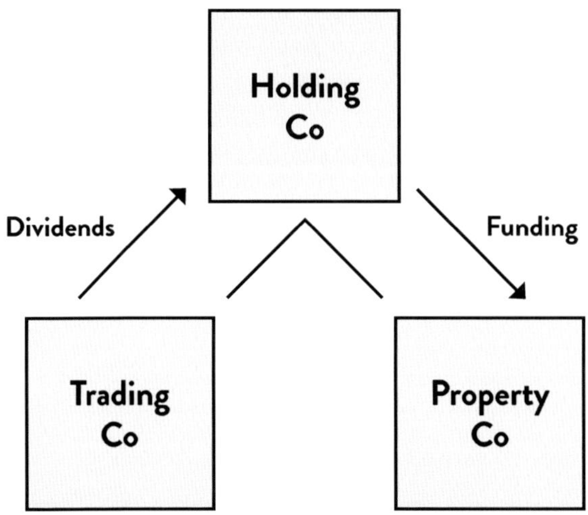

This structure provides flexibility around future sale plans and investment objectives. Typically the trading company will make profit that can then be transferred as dividends into the holding company – free of tax.

The holding company can then inject this money into the property investment subsidiary as a loan or shares for the subsidiary to start buying property.

This approach has two advantages:

- doesn't interfere with the trading company and

- allows a sale of the trading company without having to extract any valuable property beforehand (avoiding an often involved and costly process)

Process

It's advisable to get clearance from HMRC before setting up a holding company. This statutory clearance procedure means seeking confirmation from HMRC that this holding company is not being created for tax-avoidance purposes.

Benefits

There are three key benefits of the above:

1. Ability to safeguard earned profits without extracting them
2. Flexible structure for investments
3. Ability to sell trading subsidiary FREE OF TAX

Let's look at these three benefits in a little more detail.

Ability to safeguard earned profits without extracting

When your company makes profit, the resulting cash from your customers sits on the balance sheet of your company.

You then have two choices:

- withdraw this cash as your drawings / dividends or
- keep the cash in the company for working capital and reinvestment.

Withdrawing the cash into your personal name will give rise to a tax charge. Your drawings would typically be taken as dividends, incurring a top rate of tax of 38.1%.

You may not need to take the cash, in which case it builds up in the company as *retained profits*. However, you may also not want to have too much cash sitting in the company's bank account in case something unforeseen happens and the company faces claims from creditors – jeopardising the company's assets.

So how do you protect the company's cash without taking it out as a dividend?

Within a holding company structure, the trading company can vote a dividend up to the holding company which is *free of tax*.

The cash is still within a corporate entity (not in your hands personally) so you don't have to pay any income tax yet. The advantage is that it has been legally distributed out of the riskier trading company into the clean, protected holding company that your trading company's creditors can't get their hands on.

Essentially the holding company acts as your personal *war chest*, safeguarding your profits against creditors and allowing you to re-invest from the holding company into other less risky investments e.g. property.

Flexible structure for investments

Once the cash is transferred from the trading company to the holding company, it can then be re-allocated to other investments. This can be done by setting up separate 100%-owned subsidiaries of the holding company for buying property for example – as seen in the image above.

In order to fund the subsidiary's investment in property, cash can either be lent to the subsidiary or put in as share capital.

Putting the funds in as a loan offers the most flexibility because the loan can be more easily repaid. In comparison if the money is put in as share capital then it can only be called back if the shares are sold or the company wound up – or following a share buyback of some sort.

Ability to sell trading subsidiary FREE OF TAX

One potential disadvantage of the group structure is that you can lose your entitlement to Entrepreneur's Relief on the sale of your trading company. This is because you no longer hold the shares directly in the trading company to be able to sell them – the holding company now owns the shares in the trading company.

Entrepreneur's Relief reduces any tax paid on the sale of your company's shares to just 10% as opposed to 20% at the time of writing. When you sell the shares directly that are held in your name, you personally crystallise a capital gain and pay the 10% tax. The cash is then yours to do with as you please.

If the shares are held by a holding company, the sale of the trading company generates a gain for the holding company. The cash from the sale is received and belongs to the holding company – and not by you personally

The flipside, however, of having a holding company is that the sale of the trading company can be completely FREE OF TAX.

This is due to a piece of legislation known as 'Substantial Shareholding Exemption' which exempts the gain made on the sale of shares in the trading company by a holding company.

What is Substantial Shareholding Exemption?

There are conditions to meet of course; but broadly if the shares have been held for at least 12 months and the company is a trading company (rather than an investment company) then the exemption should apply.

To determine whether the holding company route is better for you than holding the shares personally, it's worth considering the following:

- Do you plan to reinvest the funds from the sale of your business into another venture or properties?
- Or would you rather have the money personally to spend / buy a new house etc?

If your answer veers towards a yes for the first question, then the holding company route could be more attractive. You keep 100% of the sale proceeds and can reinvest that sum into other ventures or properties.

If you need cash then you can draw it out as dividends in small amounts annually and limit your tax rate to the basic rate that applies to dividends.

If you did need big lump sums personally – perhaps to buy a new house, pay off a mortgage, travel the world – then it may not be as advantageous. It's worth exploring the pros and cons of each route.

OTHER ADVANTAGE OF GROUP STRUCTURES

Transfer of assets

There are several other tax advantages of operating through a group of companies. These are less well known to SMEs and tend to be exploited by large corporates and multinationals.

One of these is the ability to transfer assets e.g. property between group companies without having to pay capital gains tax or stamp duty. This can be beneficial if want to separate out properties used in the trading business for the same reasons as we've looked at already

This is typically known as an 'OpCo – PropCo' structure and can look like the below. The assets are transferred out into a fellow group company and rented back to the trading company.

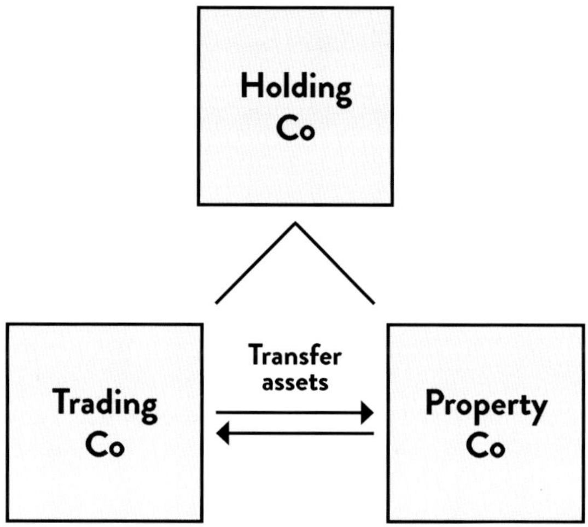

Losses

Another advantage of operating via a group is the ability to offset one company's losses against another's profits. This is known as the *Group relief* provisions.

This is especially useful if a company has made an accounting profit but after-tax adjustments may end up with a taxable loss. The taxable loss can be *surrendered* to another group company to reduce the amount of corporation tax payable by the *claimant* company.

Chapter 11

How can I reduce the amount of IHT I pay on my properties?

Death and taxes. Both inevitable.

However inheritance tax or IHT is one tax that is largely avoidable – providing planning is done in a timely manner.

Inheritance tax is levied on the value of your estate at a rate of 40% over your IHT allowance – known as the 'nil rate band'. This nil rate band is currently £325,000 per person and has been the same for a number of years.

If your estate is over £325,000, the remainder of your estate at the time of death is subject to inheritance tax at 40% and payable by your executors.

The nil rate band can increase to £500,000 if your estate consists of your family home which you are leaving for your direct descendants. However this only applies if the *total value of your estate is less than £2 million*. If it's more than this, you won't get this extra allowance.

Typically, providing you have a will, your assets are likely to pass to the surviving spouse on death. It's on the death of the remaining spouse that IHT generally kicks in.

If all assets pass to the surviving spouse, the nil rate band for the deceased spouse transfers across too. There is therefore up to £650,000 (£325,000 x 2) of IHT allowances to use against assets held at the time of death (or £1,000,000 if the estate includes the family home and total estate value is less than £2 million)

HOW CAN IHT BE REDUCED?

Without venturing into racy avoidance schemes, really there are only two ways IHT can be mitigated. Either:

1. give the asset away or

2. encumber / mortgage the asset which creates a liability against it and reduces the value of your estate.

GIVING ASSETS AWAY

You need to survive seven years after gifting the asset to avoid the IHT tax trap entirely, i.e. for the taxman not to claw it back into your estate when working out your IHT liablity.

There is some reduction after 3 years i.e. the full 40% is not applied. However the best advice is to start early.

BUT I CAN'T GIVE ASSETS AWAY AS MY CHILDREN WILL BLOW IT ALL..

That's no exaggeration and is perfectly plausible. There's a natural reticence to give everything away to the next generation for fear that they may mismanage or even squander the windfall.

Also, to some extent at least, most sensible people want their children to graft and make their own living for themselves rather than hand everything to them on a plate.

This is where Trusts can be very useful.

TRUST PLANNING

Trusts have been around for hundreds of years. They have been used mainly to give away the benefit derived from the asset while retaining legal ownership.

Trust may have been misused in recent times by promoters of tax avoidance schemes but there is absolutely no harm in using them for their intended purposes – and HMRC does not have a problem with it either.

Trusts are useful as they allow you to *give away assets whilst retaining control*. The problem is there is a limit to how much you can put into a trust without triggering a *lifetime inheritance tax charge at 20%*.

This limit is the same as the 'nil rand band' inheritance tax allowance that we *saw* earlier of £325,000 per person. You can put cash or property up to the value of £325,000 (or £650,000 per couple) into a trust without incurring any IHT.

Providing you survive seven years then it will be outside of your estate for inheritance tax purposes.

"Trusts allow you to give away assets while retaining control."

WHICH PROPERTY SHOULD I PUT INTO A TRUST?

When you transfer property into a trust, or create a declaration of trust that you are now holding the property 'on trust' for other beneficiaries i.e. children, you remain the legal owner (as Trustee).

However all benefit derived from the property, i.e. rental income or proceeds on sale, belongs to the beneficiary.

This doesn't mean you have to give away all the income or sale proceeds straight away. Depending on the type of trust you create, you can choose to pay out as much or as little income to your beneficiaries as you see fit.

The tax advantage of distributing income from the trust to the beneficiaries is that the income then becomes taxable on the beneficiary rather than you as Trustees.

This can be highly tax efficient if the beneficiaries are children and unlikely to have any other income in their name. This means they can use their personal allowances to receive the income *tax free*.

However, care is needed if the children are minors as if a parent transfers property into trust for their own minor children, the parents continue to be taxed on that income due to anti-avoidance tax rules.

On the other hand, if a grandparent or aunt/uncle does the same thing, the income is not treated as their income but is assessable on the children – thereby making use of their tax-free personal allowances.

You probably do not want to put any properties into trust if you still rely on the income that they generate.

Only assets from which you no longer need the income should be considered for transfer. Once they're into a trust and held by you as *trustee* of the trust you can no longer benefit from the income.

THE BIG ADVANTAGE

The main advantage of transferring assets (not qualifying for any IHT relief), i.e. cash or investment property, into a trust is that if you survive 7 years, you can do the same again i.e. *your nil rate band effectively renews.*

This is a little-known technique however can bring about substantial IHT savings over a lifetime by gradually shifting assets to trusts to get them out of the estate and down a generation.

Example

You and your spouse jointly own a property £650,000 in 2019. You survive seven years and in 2026 you do the same thing again. You've transferred £1.3 million into trust and out of your estate. If you survive until 2032 then *you will have saved your beneficiaries at least £520,000.*

Chapter 12

Demerger planning – how to split a portfolio tax efficiently.

There are some scenarios in which 'demerger' planning may be useful. The subject of Demergers and their tax implications is covered in UK tax legislation. Providing certain conditions are met and HMRC clearance obtained, then a demerger can provide a sensible tax solution to real-life commercial problems.

It helps to have an awareness of these scenarios so that you are not forced to sell up and pay lots of tax unnecessarily.

SO IN WHAT SITUATIONS WOULD A DEMERGER BE USEFUL?

Scenario 1

Say you have a successful trading company built up over many years. The company also used cash generated in that business to invest in property.

Now you want to sell the company but keep the properties as investments.

The properties may be commercial properties used in the trade or investment properties generating a rental return.

Either way, it's a headache trying to sell your company from both a tax perspective (Entrepreneur's Relief in question) and a commercial point of view. (Perhaps your prospective buyer doesn't want / can't afford the company *and* the properties).

Scenario 2

You have built up a property portfolio with a business partner or family member and now you have fallen out. You don't agree on the future direction of the business, making it hard for you to keep working together.

If you sell up the portfolio and divide up the cash, you will pay a lot of tax only to reinvest some of the proceeds anyway.

"A demerger can provide a sensible tax solution to real-life commercial problems."

What is a demerger?

Ordinarily trying to split properties between shareholders would give rise to significant tax charges. The transactions would have to be done at market value and therefore if shareholders were to receive their share of properties they would be subject to income tax (as a dividend) on the value of properties received.

If done correctly and in line with the legislation, a demerger can help achieve the commercial purpose without the adverse consequences.

There are several ways of using a demerger to separate property interests from the trading company or divide properties between business / partners without triggering a tax charge. Some involve using statutory reliefs and others involve voluntary liquidations.

The mechanism is fairly complex. The start and end position of a common style demerger could look like the below – the start position being two shareholders owning a half share of the assets in one company and the end position being each shareholder having their own company with their share of assets.

Start position – two shareholders, one company with all assets

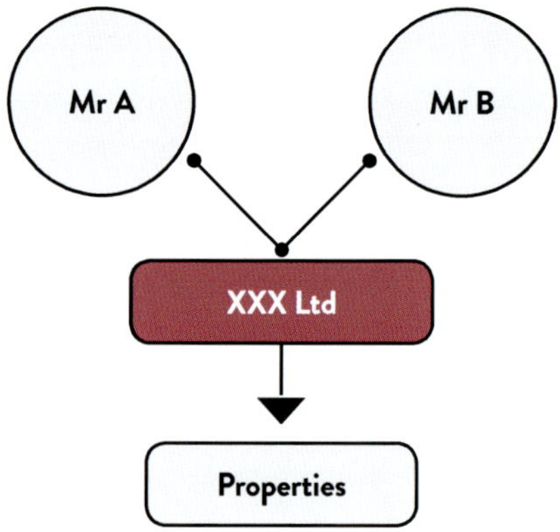

End position – two shareholders with their own company and share of assets

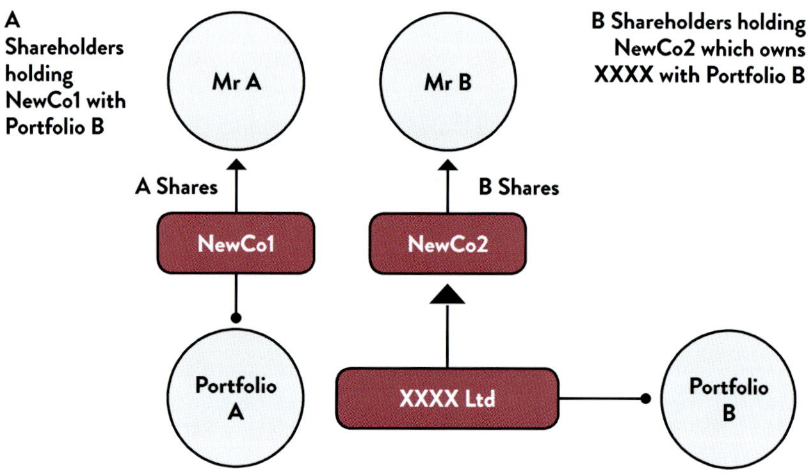

This is a highly complex area and advice should be sought before even contemplating undertaking a demerger exercise. The purpose here was to raise awareness of solutions to real life problems.

We have advised clients on demergers for this very purpose.

Case study

A client of ours – two brothers – built up a very successful property portfolio worth £15m. They got to a point where they had different ideas as to where to take the business. The older brother wanted to consolidate and tick along whilst the younger one wanted to gear up and grow.

Their tangential views were not helping the business – nor their personal relationship.

Their initial reaction was to sell the portfolio, pay off the remaining debt and split what was left to go their separate ways. In the best case scenario tax wise, that would have resulted in total tax and stamp duty of £2.85m.

We sat down and talked through the various demerger options. The demerger option would facilitate the creation of two new companies and transfer of 50% of the portfolio to each brother. They would then be free to manage, leverage and run their share of their properties as they pleased.

We managed to do this using a demerger for ZERO tax cost.

Tax efficient solution for a real life commercial problem.

Chapter 13

How should I run my serviced accommodation business?

There has been a trend in recent years to provide serviced accommodation to meet the changing habits of both travellers and millennial workers.

The Airbnb era has also spawned a growing number of home owners and second-property owners letting their properties on a short-term basis. The returns can be quite lucrative although the risk of frequent repairs and more involved management increases too.

These type of lets fall into the short-term accommodation bracket and can be further split into active trading or passive income. By active trading, I mean those businesses which set up to provide serviced accommodation either from their own properties or via others' properties i.e. via so-called 'rent to rent'.

Let's look at each type in turn.

PASSIVE INCOME

Under this heading are those who rent out their own homes via Airbnb for some of the year to generate some income; perhaps while on holiday or in between moving homes when the property is on the market.

The act of renting property out falls within the realms of taxable income and needs to be declared to HMRC – whether or not a profit is made. However, recently an allowance of £1,000 has been introduced for property income that anyone can earn before having to declare the profit to HMRC.

This allowance can also be used against other income that you may receive from your home e.g. renting out your driveway.

There is also a £1,000 property allowance that applies if you rent out your house while you are not there. This allowance can also be used against other property-related income too, for example in the case again of charging someone to park on your driveway.

If you are letting out a room in your own home (while still living there) you may qualify for the 'rent a room' relief which allows you to earn £7,500 completely tax free. This seems quite generous but can only apply if you have a lodger living with you rather than letting out the whole of your house to a third party.

PROVIDING SERVICED ACCOMMODATION

The supply of serviced accommodation has increased substantially in recent times. The relaxing of planning rules to allow offices to be converted to flats under 'permitted development' has also contributed in a rise in serviced-accommodation providers.

Moreover, with the prevalence of property networks and property entrepreneurs up and down the country sharing how they make money through property, there has come a boom in what's known as the 'rent to rent' sector.

This is a middle-man type arrangement whereby a 'rent to renter' agrees to rent a property from a landlord and guarantee rent equal to what the landlord would normally get on an assured shorthold tenancy (AST) contract.

The rent to renter then perhaps makes some minor modifications to the property to be able to rent each room out separately maybe as a house in multiple occupation (HMO) to earn a greater return.

This of course calls for more management time but the rent to renter accepts that in order to earn a profit without even having to own the property.

As a business activity it is fairly low risk and minimal investment is needed. Some landlords in a saturated market may struggle to let their properties in which case this type of offer from a rent to renter may seem lucrative.

In a similar vein, properties can be converted into short-term accommodation by rent to renters and offered on the market as serviced accommodation. Again, this can attract much higher income than a normal tenancy but, again, management is a lot more onerous and occupancy levels will fluctuate.

However as rates can be charged that are equivalent to hotel room prices the property does not need to be occupied many nights of the month to earn a return that's greater than a normal rent under an AST Contract.

HOW DOES SERVICED ACCOMMODATION DIFFER FROM A TAX PERSPECTIVE?

The main difference in the provision of serviced accommodation compared with renting a property on an Assured Shorthold Tenancy is that the supply of serviced accommodation is considered taxable from a VAT perspective.

This means that if you are providing serviced accommodation and your gross income exceeds the VAT threshold (currently £85,000) then you need to register for VAT and start charging VAT on your serviced-accommodation room rates.

By contrast, renting out residential property is always seen as an 'exempt' supply. This means that regardless of the amount of rent you receive you will never have to charge VAT on top.

IS THAT A PROBLEM?

If you need to add 20% to your room rates you will of course become that much more expensive. If your customers are mainly individuals then the VAT will be an absolute cost to them as they cannot claim it back.

Dealing with VAT compliance is another matter altogether!

But there is a way to soften the blow if you are required to register for VAT due to your gross income going over the threshold.

THE TOMS SCHEME

TOMS stands for 'Tour Operators Margin Scheme'.

It is a special VAT scheme mainly used by Tour Operators to pay VAT only on the gross margin they make on their sales as opposed to the sales themselves.

It was brought in as an EU-wide simplification measure to avoid tour operators having to register in each jurisdiction. Instead they pay output VAT on their margin not on their selling price in the country they are established rather than in the destination.

What does this have to do with serviced accommodation?

It is less well known but the TOMS VAT scheme can apply to any business which buys in and resells accommodation. Essentially this is what happens in a rent to rent arrangement – accommodation is bought from the landlord and 'resold' at a profit to the end user.

How is this beneficial?

Ordinarily you would need to declare 'output VAT' on your sales and deduct any input VAT on your purchases before arriving at the VAT to pay to HMRC every quarter.

In a rent to rent type arrangement your biggest cost is likely to be the rent paid to the landlord – which as we saw earlier is classed as 'exempt' from a VAT perspective as it relates to residential rent.

There would be no VAT on the rent paid to the landlord that could ordinarily be deducted from the VAT calculation to arrive at the VAT that's payable to HMRC. This means quite a considerable cashflow disadvantage as you need to pay all the VAT collected from your customer.

The TOMS scheme can help cashflow.

TOMS essentially allows you only to pay VAT on the margin earned i.e. income less cost of sale. The 'exempt rent' paid to the landlord can therefore be deducted from gross rents before the VAT is calculated on the 'margin' earned. That amounts to a welcome cashflow boost for rent to renters.

Chapter 14

What are the benefits of owning a Furnished Holiday Let?

If you own a holiday home that you let out for most of the year and use for your own use for some of the year then chances are it could qualify as a 'Furnished Holiday Let' (FHL) for tax purposes.

The rules were changed a few years back to make the conditions a bit more onerous. However providing you can work within the parameters below then you could qualify for some advantageous tax treatment.

WHAT QUALIFIES AS AN FHL?

A property will be treated as an FHL if the following conditions are met:

1. Property needs to be furnished
2. Property must be in the UK or EEA
3. Must be *available* for let for at least 210 days in the tax year
4. Must *actually* be let for at least 105 days or more

If your holiday home can meet the above conditions then you it can be treated as an FHL. Note that the periods of letting should be short term i.e. generally less than 30 days by any one user.

WHAT ARE THE ADVANTAGES?

One main advantage is the ability to deduct the interest paid on a loan taken out to buy the property in *full* against the rental income. With mortgage interest relief restrictions in place now for other property investments, this can be a welcome advantage.

The other main advantage is that an FHL qualifies as *business asset* as capital gains tax is concerned.

This means that a sale of an FHL benefits from being able to qualify for Entrepreneur's Relief which can reduce the tax on the gain down to just 10%. Compare this with the capital gains tax on normal residential properties which can be up to 28%.

Other capital gains tax advantages include being able to defer the gain entirely by making use of rollover relief.

This means that if the proceeds of sale on an FHL are reinvested into another business asset then the entire tax *that would normally be payable* on *the* gain can be deferred until that new asset is sold in the future.

Furthermore, given that an FHL is a business asset, it qualifies as being treated as an asset that can be transferred into Trust without an immediate capital gains tax charge by making use of deferral reliefs.

Lastly, income from FHLs are considered as *earnings* from an income tax perspective. This is helpful for pension contribution purposes if your pension contributions made personally cannot be more than your 'earnings'. Rents from other residential properties and dividends do not qualify as earnings.

Thank you for reading this book

I hope there has been something in it that has helped answer your property related questions.

If you found it useful and the book has helped you in some way, I would be very grateful if you could hop on over to Amazon and leave a short review.

What next?

This book is intended to give you an awareness of the myriad of issues surrounding property taxes and give you a steer as to how to be more tax efficient. You should always seek professional advice from an expert on your personal circumstances as tax is always changing and your advisor needs to understand your individual position.

If you would like some advice from me on your specific affairs then please go to page 14 to see how you can arrange a Strategic Consultation.

More about the Author

Reza started his career with PwC in Birmingham – the largest accountancy firm in the world (at the time) – where he qualified as a chartered accountant and chartered tax advisor. He progressed to managing a portfolio of Entrepreneur and Owner-Managed Business clients and advising them on their corporate and personal tax affairs.

In 2008 the opportunity came to buy into a small firm on the South Coast called Walji & Co. Reza has since grown the firm three-fold and carved out a specialism in advising clients on property related matters.

Coupled with his tax expertise on property, he is also actively involved in property investment and development projects on a personal level. This practical experience together with the tax know-how leave him well positioned to advise clients on structuring, managing, growing and selling their property related interests in a tax efficient manner.

He also has a passion for helping entrepreneurs and business owners transform their profits to achieve their personal goals (rather than just crunching the numbers) and has written a book on the subject called 'Transform Your Profits through Price'. More details can be found at www.transformyourprofits.co.uk

Outside of his work, Reza has played an active role as Trustee for several charities contributing his expertise to help the charities achieve their financial self-sufficiency goals.

At home he is kept busy as a father of four young children but must make time for visiting the gym at least 3-4 times a week!

You can connect with Reza on Linkedin or can send him an email directly at: reza@walji.uk.com

More about his firm Walji & Co at www.walji.uk.com

Reza Hooda, FCA CTA
Property Tax Expert & Investor